WIMBLEDON

by Marty Gitlin

Published by ABDO Publishing Company, PO Box 398166, Minneapolis, MN 55439. Copyright © 2013 by Abdo Consulting Group, Inc. International copyrights reserved in all countries. No part of this book may be reproduced in any form without written permission from the publisher. SportsZone™ is a trademark and logo of ABDO Publishing Company.

Printed in the United States of America,
North Mankato, Minnesota
102012
012013

Editor: Chrös McDougall
Series Designer: Craig Hinton

Photo Credits: Kirsty Wigglesworth/AP Images, Cover, 11, 52, 59 (bottom, right); Adam Stoltman/AP Images, Title, 44, 60 (center); Anja Niedringhaus/AP Images, 5, 55, 57; Ian Walton/AP Images, 7; Hulton Archive/Getty Images, 13, 25, 58 (top, left), 59 (top); Popperfoto/Getty Images, 16, 58 (top, right); Press Association/AP Images, 19; Corbis Bettmann/AP Images, 23, 33, 60 (top); AP Images, 29, 30, 37, 39; Peter Kemp/AP Images, 35; Walter Iooss Jr. /Sports Illustrated/Getty Images, 41; Bob Dear/AP Images, 47, 58 (bottom); Rui Vieira/AP Images, 50, 59 (bottom, left); AELTC / Tom Lovelock/AFP/Getty Images, 60 (bottom)

Cataloging-in-Publication Data
Gitlin, Marty.
 Wimbledon / Marty Gitlin.
   p. cm. -- (Sports' great championships)
Includes bibliographical references and index.
ISBN 978-1-61783-674-9
1. Tennis--History--Juvenile literature. 2. Wimbledon Championships--History--Juvenile literature.
I. Title.
796.343--dc22

                                                                          2012946246

TABLE OF CONTENTS

Thriller on Centre Court

One point. That was all Rafael Nadal needed. One point and he would win his first Wimbledon tennis tournament. One point and he would end the reign of Roger Federer, perhaps the greatest player in the history of the sport. One point and he would deny Federer a record sixth straight Wimbledon crown.

It was July 6, 2008. The Centre Court stands at the All England Club were packed. Millions of television viewers around the world were spellbound. They had seen Nadal win two of the first three sets in the

Roger Federer battles Rafael Nadal during their epic men's final at Wimbledon in 2008.

Men's tennis in the United States had been declining for several years by 2008. That was reflected at Wimbledon. No American won the men's title from 2001 to 2012. The only one to reach the finals was Andy Roddick, who lost to Federer in 2004, 2005, and 2009. That was quite a change from the previous decade. Pete Sampras dominated Wimbledon in the 1990s. He captured the title every year but one from 1993 to 2000. Fellow American Andre Agassi won it in 1992.

best-of-five match. They watched the two superstars battle to a 6–6 tie in the fourth set to force a tiebreaker. They watched Nadal slam a brilliant forehand winner to place himself on the brink of the title.

It was match point. Nadal blasted his serve and rushed to the net. He smacked a topspin forehand that forced Federer to race to his left and hit a backhand. Some felt Federer had a weak backhand. But there was nothing weak about this one. Federer hit it with force. It landed within a foot of the line. Nadal could only watch in frustration as it whizzed past him for a point.

Federer lived on. And soon he was smashing an ace serve to win the fourth set. The winner of the fifth set would be Wimbledon champion. One of the greatest moments in the history of tennis' most historic tournament was about to begin.

Rafael Nadal returns a shot against Roger Federer during their 2008 Wimbledon men's final.

Clash of the Champions

Wimbledon is the oldest and, some say, most prestigious tennis tournament in the world. Fans expected the 2008 final to be an all-time classic battle from the start. Federer and Nadal had proved to be the best players in the world. They boasted contrasting styles. Federer was a power hitter with great all-around skills. He could beat opponents by blasting hard, spinning serves, hitting strong baseline shots, and by rushing to the net for winning volleys. Federer hoped to win points quickly.

Nadal liked to stay back at the baseline and let balls bounce. He rarely made mistakes. When Federer came to the net, Nadal tried to slam the ball past him.

After two sets on this rainy day at Wimbledon in south London, few thought the match would stretch all the way to a fifth set. Nadal had won the first two sets by 6–4 scores. Federer had jumped to a 4–1 lead in the second set. But Nadal then won five straight games to take the set. He appeared unbeatable. He seemed certain to become the first player since Bjorn Borg in 1980 to win the French Open and Wimbledon in back-to-back years.

But Federer refused to surrender his title without a fight. He clinched the third set tiebreaker with an ace. He had all the momentum when he won the fourth set in a tiebreaker as well.

Soon Mother Nature stepped in. The third rain delay of the day stopped play. Many wondered if it would become too dark to finish. But the players returned to the court about 30 minutes later to finish their match.

Marathon Match

As the rivals matched brilliant shots, it became the longest final in Wimbledon history. Federer had his chance to win the match. Leading 5–4 in the fifth set, he needed just two points to earn his sixth straight Wimbledon crown. But Nadal came back and tied it.

Normally a set goes to a tiebreaker at this point. But Wimbledon rules force players to win the fifth set by two games. So Federer and Nadal played on. And they continued to hold serve while it became darker and harder to see. If the match lasted much longer, it would have to be finished the following day. Federer nearly asked for it to be postponed.

Nadal tried his best to end it before darkness made it impossible to continue. He forced a forehand mistake to break Federer's serve and take an 8–7 lead. But Federer again refused to give in. Nadal earned three championship points, but Federer won all of them to stay alive. Nadal finally clinched victory when Federer hit a forehand into the net.

After 4 hours and 48 minutes of tennis, Nadal had captured his first Wimbledon title. He had won the most coveted title in the sport. The Spaniard collapsed to the ground as the fans cheered and hailed the new champion.

Venus Out of This World

The 2008 Wimbledon men's final was perhaps the greatest tennis match ever played. But the women also put on a great show that year. Zheng Jie became the first Chinese player to reach the Wimbledon semifinals. Then sisters Venus and Serena Williams battled it out for the title.

That was nothing new. The Williams sisters had already met 15 times during their careers, with Serena winning eight times and Venus seven. They even played for the Wimbledon crown four times. In 2002, 2003, and 2009, Serena won. But Venus got her revenge in 2008. She overcame a 4–2 deficit in the first set in the best-of-three match. Then she won the last two games of the second set to earn the title. But Venus did not celebrate after winning. She did not want to hurt her sister's feelings.

Just hours after battling each other, they battled together. The Williams sisters teamed up to win the Wimbledon women's doubles final.

He climbed through the stands to embrace family members. He greeted the royal family of his native Spain. He was proud to become the first Spaniard in 42 years to win the Wimbledon men's singles title.

"It's impossible to explain what I felt in that moment," Nadal said. "I'm very, very happy. It is a dream to play on this court, my favorite tournament, but I never imagined this."

The sight of Nadal celebrating contrasted with Federer looking dejected. He had never finished second at Wimbledon. He could take pride in knowing he had lost an epic match in history. But he never felt such pain after a defeat.

After nearly five hours of tennis, Rafael Nadal finally beat Roger Federer in the 2008 Wimbledon final. Nadal became the first Spaniard in 42 years to win the title.

"Probably my hardest loss, by far," said a badly shaken Federer. "I mean it's not much harder than this is right now. I'm disappointed, and I'm crushed. [Nadal] played a super match, and I'm sure it was a great match to watch and to play, but it's all over now."

Federer had lost to Nadal many times before. So why did he feel such emotion? Because he had never lost to Nadal at Wimbledon. He also understood that Wimbledon is special. It boasts more tradition than any other tournament. Tennis players have been aware of that for more than 100 years.

The Early World of Wimbledon

I t was a rainy July 19, 1877, in England. A British cricket player named Spencer Gore had just won the first Wimbledon title. A crowd of 200 fans dressed in their finest clothes to watch. But one man was not impressed with tennis played on grass. That man was Spencer Gore.

He said it was "doubtful" that any player would "ever seriously give his attention to lawn tennis."

He had good reason for his doubt. After all, the first Wimbledon was played only to raise money to keep the croquet lawns in good shape at

the All England Croquet Club. Of course Wimbledon, which is also known simply as the Championships, grew into one of the most famous sporting events in the world. And its millions of fans have Major Walter Clopton Wingfield to thank for it.

Wingfield was a retired army officer. He wanted to create a game for friends and family. So he laid out a court on his estate. It was shaped like an hourglass with a net in the middle. Then he wrote out a set of rules.

Wingfield introduced his game at a party in December 1873. He patented it in February 1874 and called it "Sphairistike." The word was Greek for "skill in playing at ball."

The name of the game was not popular. But the game itself was. The All England Croquet Club soon added lawn tennis to its list of activities. The club changed the shape of the court to a rectangle. In 1877 it changed its name to the All England Lawn Tennis and Croquet Club, or All England Club for short. But most of the rules set forth by Wingfield have remained in today's game.

Soon the sport was being played in the United States as well. But the center of the lawn tennis world was Wimbledon, an area south of London.

The 1877 tournament was limited to men (the tournament refers to men as gentlemen). It did not take long for the first stars to emerge. Twin brothers William and Ernest Renshaw took the event by storm in the 1880s. They were the first to blast aces. They beat foes by rushing to the net and slamming winning volleys.

Fans flocked to see the Renshaws play during the 1880s. William won the Wimbledon title every year from 1881 to 1886. It became obvious that power players would rule on the grass courts, where balls bounce faster. That fact remains true today.

More Brilliant Brothers

Another set of English brothers soon took over. Reginald and Laurie Doherty combined to win all but one Wimbledon singles crown from 1897 to 1906. Reginald won four straight from 1897 to 1900. Laurie took five in a row from 1902 to 1906. No men's player matched that streak until Bjorn Borg from 1976 to 1980. Some consider the Doherty brothers the first tennis idols.

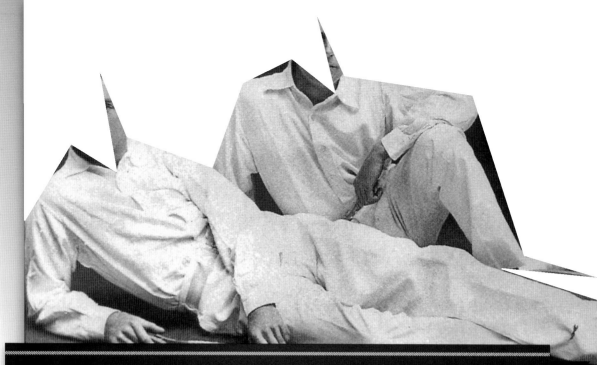

English brothers Reginald and Laurie Doherty starred at Wimbledon around the turn of the nineteenth century. They won every men's title from 1897 to 1906.

"They were the game's first superstars," wrote former British tennis player John Barrett. "[They were] a handsome and cultured pair whose dress, deportment, and modest manner . . . created a new following for the lawn tennis."

Strangely, the Doherty brothers clashed only once for the Wimbledon title. Reginald beat Laurie in an epic five-set match in 1898.

A women's (known at Wimbledon as ladies') competition was added to Wimbledon in 1884. The first women's star of Wimbledon arrived a few years later. Lottie Dod was just 15 when she won her first championship

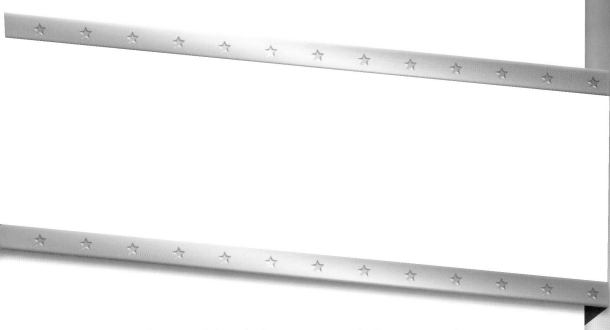

in 1897. She earned the title four more times before quitting the sport. Dod said she had become bored with winning so easily.

Wimbledon had long been limited to British players. The addition of international players in 1901 made the tournament field stronger. The British men and women won for a few more years. American May Sutton won the 1905 women's title, and in 1907 Australian Norman Brookes was the first non-British player to win the men's tournament. Wimbledon had become truly international.

That marked the end of British rule in the tournament. But the tennis stars who graced the Wimbledon courts attracted huge crowds. It seemed the men and women took turns grabbing the spotlight.

The All England Club

The All England Croquet Club opened in 1868. Now known as the All England Lawn Tennis and Croquet Club, it has been home to Wimbledon since the tournament's beginning. Although the club has several grass tennis courts, many of which are used year-round, the focal point is Centre Court. It was originally named for its location in the grounds. However, after the club moved to its current location in 1922, it was no longer in the direct center. Still, the biggest matches—including the finals—continue to take place on Centre Court. The stadium surrounding it seats nearly 14,000 fans. A retractable roof was added to the stadium in 2009 to combat bad weather in rainy London.

The first great champion of the twentieth century was Tony Wilding. The dashing and handsome player from New Zealand rode around Europe on a motorcycle. He earned four straight Wimbledon singles titles from 1910 to 1913. He might have won more, but he was killed in World War I. Wilding served as a pilot for the British air force.

Wilding was soon outdone by Suzanne Lenglen of France. Lenglen burst onto the scene in 1919 by beating seven-time singles champion Dorothea Chambers in the final. Lenglen twice survived match point in the third set in a 10–8, 4–6, 9–7 victory.

That was the first of five titles in a row for Lenglen. She destroyed foes with pinpoint accuracy. She went on to be one of the finest female

The All England Lawn Tennis and Croquet Club has been in its current location since 1922. Centre Court added a retractable roof in 2009.

players in tennis history. After beating Chambers, she dominated events from beginning to end. Even her matches in the Wimbledon finals were rarely close. Lenglen held her finals opponents to a combined 11 games in winning every title match from 1920 to 1923. She also won in 1925.

"She played with marvelous ease," said French men's tennis star Rene Lacoste. "[She had] the simplest strokes in the world."

Four Fine Frenchmen

Lacoste was a champion in his own right. He was the finest player among a group of Frenchmen known as "The Four Musketeers." Lacoste, Henri Cochet, Jean Borotra, and Jacques Brugnon dominated Wimbledon during their era.

Lacoste, Cochet, and Borotra combined to win it every year from 1924 to 1929. The Four Musketeers did not always like each other. But they were proud to represent France.

"They were all very different . . . and they sometimes clashed bitterly with one another on the courts," wrote Wimbledon secretary Duncan Macaulay. "But whenever they felt they were playing for France, they always put France first."

While the Four Musketeers were winning title after title, one great US woman was doing the same. Helen Wills Moody never changed expression on the court. But she had plenty to smile about. She won every singles crown from 1927 to 1930. She slammed the ball with greater force than any female player of her era. Moody finished her incredible career with eight Wimbledon singles championships.

Wimbledon's popularity motivated the All England Club to find it a bigger home. The club bought a plot of nearby land after World War I. A new Centre Court was built with seating for 11,000 fans. It opened in 1922 and remains Wimbledon's home. The move seemed to bring bad luck at the first tournament that year. It rained every day on the Wimbledon courts.

The level of talent at Wimbledon also grew during the 1920s and 1930s. Some of the best players in the world could not win consistently. Among them was Bill Tilden of the United States.

Tilden won the singles title in 1920 and 1921. He boasted

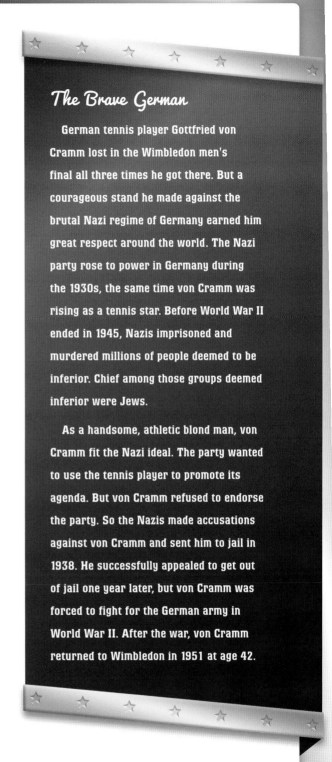

The Brave German

German tennis player Gottfried von Cramm lost in the Wimbledon men's final all three times he got there. But a courageous stand he made against the brutal Nazi regime of Germany earned him great respect around the world. The Nazi party rose to power in Germany during the 1930s, the same time von Cramm was rising as a tennis star. Before World War II ended in 1945, Nazis imprisoned and murdered millions of people deemed to be inferior. Chief among those groups deemed inferior were Jews.

As a handsome, athletic blond man, von Cramm fit the Nazi ideal. The party wanted to use the tennis player to promote its agenda. But von Cramm refused to endorse the party. So the Nazis made accusations against von Cramm and sent him to jail in 1938. He successfully appealed to get out of jail one year later, but von Cramm was forced to fight for the German army in World War II. After the war, von Cramm returned to Wimbledon in 1951 at age 42.

the power to succeed on the grass at Wimbledon. But he struggled for years after that initial success. He lost in the semifinals three times. He did not win another Wimbledon crown until age 37 in 1930. Yet he won seven US Championship titles from 1920 to 1929. The US Championship is now known as the US Open.

Great players continued to grace the Wimbledon courts. Fred Perry of England won three men's singles titles during the 1930s. Don Budge of the United States won two.

But England had far more serious matters to consider as the decade progressed. Germany was preparing to wage war in Europe. World War II began in Europe in September 1939. No tennis balls would bounce again on the Wimbledon courts until 1946.

Two countries dominated play when the event did return. The Australian men were about to take control. So were the US women. A new era of Wimbledon was about to begin.

New Breed of Superstar

The Wimbledon courts suffered greatly from enemy bombing during World War II. Five German bombs fell on Centre Court during a raid in October 1940. But the grounds were ready when the event resumed in 1946. And so was Louise Brough of California, who emerged as the most dominant player in the sport.

Brough won three straight championships from 1948 to 1950. She twice lost in the finals before snagging the crown again in 1955. She also won five titles in women's doubles. Unlike many female players of her

Louise Brough of the United States won four Wimbledon women's singles and five doubles titles between 1946 and 1955.

generation, Brough used a power game to beat foes. She rushed the net after serving and looked to hit volley winners.

Her early run of titles was stopped by another Californian known as "Little Mo." Tiny and pretty Maureen Connolly was the darling of the tennis scene. Fans embraced her friendly and outgoing personality. Her style on the court contrasted that of Brough. Connolly remained on the baseline and frustrated foes with hard and precise shots. She won her first Wimbledon singles title at age of 17 in 1952.

Connolly was just warming up. She won the next two championships and seemed destined to dominate for years. But her career ended at age 19 when her right leg was crushed in a horseback riding accident. She was remembered as one of the great tennis players in history. "With her perfect timing . . . balance and confidence, [Connolly] has developed the most powerful stroke of its kind the game has known," reporter Allison Danzig wrote of Connolly in the *New York Times*.

More American Mastery

Connolly never played competitive tennis again. But US women kept rolling on Centre Court. The most notable was Althea Gibson, the first black tennis star. Gibson was known as "the Jackie Robinson of tennis." Robinson excelled as the first black Major League Baseball player in 1947. Gibson followed his example, winning Wimbledon titles in 1957 and 1958.

While the United States was ruling women's tennis, a country halfway around the world was dominating the men's game. Australia produced champion after champion from 1956 to 1971.

The training of young tennis players in Australia began paying off in the early 1950s. Every year from 1950 to 1953 it won the Davis Cup. That is an annual men's tennis competition among national teams from around the world. Australians were on their way to capturing 15 Davis Cup crowns in a span of 18 years. Soon they were ready to rule Wimbledon as well.

The great champions just kept appearing on Centre

Teaming Up for Titles

It takes a special bond and talent to thrive in doubles. It requires a great ability to work with a teammate. Great doubles players boast excellent skills at the net and on the baseline. Many premier doubles players at Wimbledon did not excel in singles. That is why some of the greatest doubles players are not very famous.

Jacques Brugnon was the most obscure player among the famed French Four Musketeers. But he was the best in doubles. Brugnon teamed up with Henri Cochet and Jean Borotra to win four doubles titles during the 1920s and 1930s.

Australian Todd Woodbridge was hardly competitive in singles, but he won an amazing nine doubles championships with two different partners from 1993 to 2004.

There were exceptions. American great John McEnroe and Australian star John Newcombe both won singles and doubles crowns. So did female singles stars Suzanne Lenglen, Billie Jean King, and Martina Navratilova.

Court. During one 16-year period, six Australians won Wimbledon titles and four others lost to them in the finals. Lew Hoad, Roy Emerson, Rod Laver, and John Newcombe all captured more than one Wimbledon championship.

The finest of all was Laver. The muscular left-hander was arguably the greatest player in tennis history. He remained the only two-time winner of the Grand Slam through 2011. The Grand Slam is earned by winning the Australian Open, the French Open, Wimbledon, and the US Open in the same year.

The redhead won Wimbledon titles four times during the 1960s. He could have won more had he not played professional tennis from 1963 to 1967. Wimbledon, like most tennis tournaments, was limited to amateur players until 1968.

With four singles titles, Australia's Rod Laver was the most successful of many great Australians at Wimbledon during the 1960s.

Many believe Laver had no flaws in his game. Among those who believed he was the best ever was Tony Trabert, a star player who later became a tennis analyst. Trabert argued that winning a Grand Slam as both an amateur and professional made Laver the best ever. Trabert made that claim in 2008, after great champions such as Bjorn Borg, Jimmy Connors, John McEnroe, and Roger Federer had starred on Centre Court.

"If someone in some sport held a world record that no one else had, you would say that person was the best in that sport," Trabert said. "So in my view, you've got to say Laver is the best of all time."

Billie Jean King of the United States helped usher in a new era of great tennis popularity during the 1960s and 1970s.

Billie Jean King of the United States emerged during the same period. She won all four Grand Slam tournaments during her storied career, but King especially dominated at Wimbledon. King used an attacking style to win six singles titles. She also won 10 doubles titles and four mixed doubles titles. King had a fierce will to win. She admitted that she hated to lose because she would always remember defeat.

"Victory is fleeting," she said. "Losing is forever."

Losing for no money is even tougher. The tennis world was changing in the 1960s. And so was Wimbledon. Tennis had long been a rich

"Battle of the Sexes"

Tennis entered its most popular period during the 1970s. A big reason for that was the 1973 "Battle of the Sexes," when former men's star Bobby Riggs challenged women's star Billie Jean King to a match. It was a time when women around the world were fighting for equality. Riggs claimed that no woman could beat a man on the court. A crowd of 30,000 fans showed up at the Houston Astrodome to attend the showdown. Millions of television viewers witnessed the event. They watched as King dominated Riggs in three straight sets. The attention given to the match set off an explosion of popularity for the sport.

person's game. As such, many players did not need the sport to support themselves. So for many years it was looked down upon for players to accept money for winning Wimbledon or other tennis tournaments.

That attitude began to change. Players sometimes received money in secret. Others entered professional events to make money. However, once a player became a professional, he or she could no longer play at Wimbledon and the other Grand Slams.

More players began protesting by the 1960s. Thousands of fans were paying money to watch them play. They felt they should receive their fair share. And in 1968, they got their wish. The "Open Era" of tennis was about to begin. Soon all four Grand Slams—and most of the tennis world—were open to professionals.

Tennis Boom Begins

The Open Era gave a greater sense of power to the players. In 1973, Nikki Pilic was suspended by his native Yugoslavia for refusing to participate in the Davis Cup. Wimbledon honored the action and banned Pilic from playing in its tournament.

That angered his fellow players. Nearly 100 men's players boycotted Wimbledon that year. Little-known Jan Kodes won the event. That helped tennis players form unions to represent their interests.

The changes that came with the Open Era ultimately brought great popularity to the sport. Much of that came from the players themselves. Throughout the sport's history, most of the players came from wealthy families. There had always been a polite nature to the sport. But the Open

John McEnroe kicks his racket during a match at Wimbledon in 1980. The US player was one of many players who showed a lot of emotion on the court at this time.

Era introduced tennis to a more diverse audience. Players became more independent, outspoken, and, in some cases, rude. But the fans loved it.

Brash young players such as Connors and McEnroe of the United States screamed at officials and threw their rackets in anger. They were also among the greatest players in the world. Not all players acted like that, though. Other young stars such as Stan Smith, Arthur Ashe, and Bjorn Borg were known for their politeness.

Meanwhile, new women's stars Chris Evert and Martina Navratilova brought excitement as they competed with established greats Margaret Court and King. Wimbledon was becoming more thrilling than ever.

The Boom Era

It was July 6, 1974. Millions of Americans had enjoyed watching the Independence Day fireworks two nights earlier. Now they were being treated to some fireworks on television. They were witnessing the Wimbledon men's singles final.

The fireworks were coming in the form of explosive baseline shots. Battling for the crown were veteran Australian Ken Rosewall and young, upstart US player Jimmy Connors. But this match was no battle at all. It was one of the most lopsided title matches in Wimbledon history.

Jimmy Connors was known for his great tennis skills as well as his occasional outbursts on the court.

Upset of the Decade

The 1975 Wimbledon men's final was a picture of contrast. Jimmy Connors was white, bold, and 22 years old. Arthur Ashe was black, polite, and nearly 32. Connors was a superstar and regarded as the best player in the world. Ashe was an above-average player, but past his prime.

The two US players did not get along. When Connors refused to play for the United States in the Davis Cup, Ashe claimed he was unpatriotic. Connors was also angered when the Association of Tennis Professionals (ATP) banned him from playing in the French Open. Ashe was president of the ATP. The ban was the result of Connors joining a new US league called World Team Tennis.

So there was great tension when Ashe and Connors clashed for the 1975 crown. Most believed Connors would win easily. But Ashe kept him off-balance by changing the pace of his shots. It was no contest. Ashe won easily to become the first black male singles champion at Wimbledon.

Connors dominated from beginning to end for a 6–1, 6–1, 6–4 victory.

Other championship matches were far more exciting. But this one ushered in a new era. It featured a contrast between young and old, the past and future of tennis. Rosewall was 39 and on his way out. Connors was 21 and an intense kid who had taken the sport by storm.

When he finished off Rosewall, Connors tossed his racket into the air. He had been dreaming of capturing the Wimbledon title since he was six. He thought to himself that he might never win it again. And he started to cry.

Arthur Ashe shocked many when he upset fellow American Jimmy Connors to win the Wimbledon men's singles title in 1975.

The woman to which Connors was engaged had also shed such tears of joy the day before. That pony-tailed star was Chris Evert, who cried after easily winning her first Wimbledon title.

Evert was nothing like Connors. She was quiet on the court. She showed little emotion. She rarely complained. He was cocky. He displayed both joy and rage. He often voiced his anger when calls went against him.

Evert and Connors represented a new era in tennis. It seemed brilliant young players emerged every year. Millions of new fans eagerly awaited

Marathon Match

It took two days to complete the match between 41-year-old legend Pancho Gonzales and Charlie Pasarell in 1969. Wimbledon did not allow tiebreakers until 1979. Players before that had to win sets by at least two games. The result was a first set that lasted an incredible 46 games. Gonzales lost the first set as well as the second before bouncing back to win the next three sets. The final score was 22–24, 1–6, 16–14, 6–3, 11–9. The match was halted and completed the next day. It lasted more than five hours.

showdowns between the best of the best. And Wimbledon remained the center of the tennis universe.

Sweet-Stroking Swede

Connors continued to win championships. But not at Wimbledon, at least for several years. The men's event was soon being dominated by a long-haired Swedish star named Bjorn Borg. The handsome blond boasted the same personality as Evert. He neither smiled nor frowned on the court. He simply stayed on the baseline and carved up opponents with precise ground strokes.

The Wimbledon grass favors power players. Those who blast hard serves and attack the net most often enjoy the greatest success. But Borg

Bjorn Borg of Sweden won five Wimbledon men's singles titles in a row from 1976 to 1980. That matched Laurie Doherty's streak from the early 1900s.

was the opposite. He waited for others to rush the net. Then he slammed the ball past them. He was simply a magician with a racket in his hand.

Borg embarked on the greatest run of singles success at Wimbledon in 70 years. He won four straight titles from 1976 to 1979, beating Connors in the finals twice along the way. But it was his shot at a fifth crown in a row that produced one of the most memorable matches that had ever been played.

It was the 1980 final. Borg's opponent was John McEnroe. The young US player made Connors seem tame. McEnroe yelled at officials and opponents. He threw his racket to the ground. And when he was booed by fans, he played better. His anger was matched only by his great skills as a tennis player.

That brilliance was on display when he needed it the most. McEnroe was on the brink of defeat with the 1980 title on the line. He had lost two of the first three sets to Borg. They battled in an epic fourth-set tiebreaker. Borg had seven match points, but McEnroe won them all to stay alive. However, McEnroe then lost all five points that would have forced a fifth set. The result was an incredible 16–16 score in the tiebreaker.

Then McEnroe slammed a serve to Borg's forehand and rushed the net. Borg tried to blast it past him, but missed. McEnroe had earned his sixth set point. This time he did not fail. He won the set when Borg missed an easy forehand. The two were headed for a fifth and deciding set.

Bjorn Borg falls to the grass in celebration after beating John McEnroe in the famous 1980 Wimbledon men's final. It was his fifth title in a row.

The always confident McEnroe figured he was about to win his first Wimbledon crown. "I knew I had won the match," he said. "I *knew* it."

He was not alone. "That was the toughest moment in my tennis career. " Borg said. "I knew John thought he would win the match. I thought he would win the match. I don't know how I regrouped."

But Borg did regroup. He was as tough as nails. His stoic nature did not allow him to fall apart. He won every service game in the fifth set. Soon he was hoisting the championship trophy for the fifth straight year.

McEnroe, Borg, and Connors won every Wimbledon singles title from 1976 to 1984. The rivalries they forged proved legendary. And so did the battles between Evert and upstart Martina Navratilova, who would go on to win a record 20 total Wimbledon titles.

Classic Showdown

Finals featuring Navratilova and Evert were a regular event from 1978 to 1985. The two clashed for the crown five times during that period. The grass courts favored the hard-hitting Navratilova, and it showed. She won all five meetings.

Their most famous meeting was their first, in 1978. Navratilova was full of emotion that day. She yearned to play in front of her family, but it was impossible. She had moved from Czechoslovakia to the United States in 1975 and had not seen her parents or sister since. The Communist government of Czechoslovakia would not allow Navratilova's family to leave the country.

The two stars split the first two sets. Evert led 4–2 in the third set and appeared on her way to a third Wimbledon title. But Navratilova fought off three match points to stay alive. She then won 12 of the last 13 points to clinch the championship.

It was a bittersweet moment. She was thrilled to win her first Wimbledon title. Her parents drove to the German border to watch

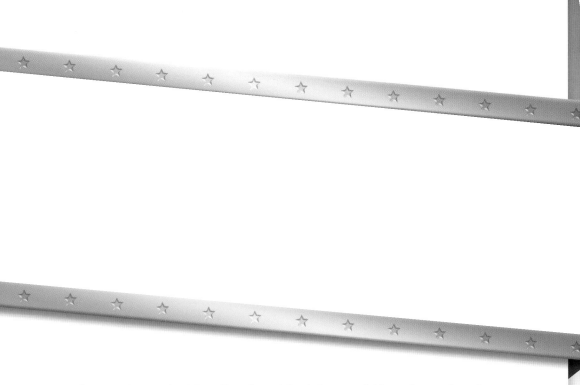

the match on television. But she wished they could have been there in person.

"I don't know if I should cry or scream or laugh," she said. "I feel very happy that I won, but at the same time I'm very sad that I can't share this with my family."

Navratilova beat Evert in the finals in 1979, 1982, 1984, and 1985. And she just kept on winning. By the time she had stopped blasting serves and volleys past her opponents, she had won nine Wimbledon singles championships. No male or female player has matched it through 2012. Navratilova also won seven Wimbledon doubles titles and four

mixed doubles titles. That tied her with Billie Jean King for the most total Wimbledon titles—by a man or woman—with 20.

Meanwhile, times were changing in men's tennis. McEnroe beat Connors easily for the Wimbledon championship in 1984. That was the last time either of them reached the finals. Another new era was about to begin.

That new era featured a US man who dominated Wimbledon in the 1990s. It also spotlighted two US sisters who took turns winning titles in the decade that followed. Some of the most exciting matches in Wimbledon history were yet to come.

Pete, Roger, and the Sister Stars

T he champions of Wimbledon in the late 1980s did not have to travel far from home to get there. Europeans had much more success at the time than players from the United States.

John McEnroe and Jimmy Connors were no longer the greatest players in the game. Neither were Chris Evert and Martina Navratilova, who was now a US citizen. Instead, German Boris Becker and Swede Stefan Edberg were the leaders among the men. And German Steffi Graf was ruling the women's game.

Steffi Graf returns a shot against Martina Navratilova during the 1988 Wimbledon women's singles final en route to claiming her first Wimbledon championship.

Graf was all but unbeatable into the mid-1990s. She played her first Wimbledon at age 15 in 1984. She won seven titles from 1988 to 1996. Many believe her forehand was one of the best ever seen on Centre Court. Her speed and quickness allowed her to track down shots others could never reach.

Navratilova remained a force until the late 1980s, when Graf stepped to the forefront. The two clashed in the finals in 1988 and 1989. Graf won both matches in three sets to secure the number-one ranking in the world. She was all but unbeatable in 1988. She not only captured the rare Grand Slam, but also won a gold medal in the summer Olympic Games.

This period was disappointing for those who hoped to see deep runs by US players. No US man qualified for the finals from 1986 to 1991. Only one US woman appeared at Centre Court with the title on the line from 1991 to 1998.

The sport was declining in popularity in the United States. US fans needed a homegrown star. And they got two in Pete Sampras and Andre Agassi. The two young players began a rivalry in the early 1990s that lasted a decade. But there was no doubt as to who was superior at Wimbledon. It was Sampras.

It seemed Sampras's style and talent were made for the grass courts of Wimbledon. He boasted a powerful forehand, precision volley, and a rocket of a serve. He overpowered foe after foe.

Meeting His Match

One opponent even Sampras could not overpower was Croatian Goran Ivanisevic. Ivanisevic blasted his serve and played the same power style as Sampras. The two slammed ace after ace past each other when they played. It was almost impossible for either to break serve.

They met in one of the most famous title showdowns ever in 1998. Sampras had already won four of the previous five Wimbledon men's singles titles. He was expected to win easily. After all, he was the number-one player in the world. Ivanisevic was only ranked number 25.

Defending Wimbledon champion Pete Sampras reaches for a shot against Goran Ivanisevic during the 1998 men's singles final.

But Ivanisevic was on top of his game. He slammed one ace after another past Sampras to win the first set. Sampras then took control. He won the next two sets and appeared to be cruising to victory. Ivanisevic refused to give up. He blasted four passing shots by Sampras to break serve and win the fourth set. Sampras was sweating it out.

"In the fifth set, there were these thoughts: 'Oh, my god, if I lose, how am I going to feel?'" Sampras recalled. "I have an unbelievable fear of losing. That's what gets me going."

Sweet Treat and Tradition

The most famous food associated with Wimbledon is strawberries and cream. Fans have been eating the sweet treat there since the event began in 1877. The tournament and strawberries both arrive at the same time early in the summer. "Strawberries were normally available only at that time of year," explained Wimbledon Lawn Tennis Museum librarian Audrey Snell. "When [Wimbledon] began . . . it was a fashionable thing to eat."

The fear quickly drained away. Sampras dominated the rest of the match. Ivanisevic's powerful serve did not seem so powerful anymore. Sampras broke his serve twice in the fifth set to clinch another Wimbledon crown. He finished his career with seven Wimbledon titles. That matched William Renshaw for the most in the history of the men's event.

The Williams Sisters

The day before Sampras captured his last championship, a new era began in women's singles at Wimbledon. It was 2000 when two African-American sisters began dominating on Centre Court. Venus and Serena Williams boasted the ideal games for winning on grass.

In addition to their combined 10 Wimbledon singles titles, Serena, *left*, and Venus Williams have combined to win five Wimbledon doubles titles through 2012.

They were big, strong, fast, and hard-hitting. They overpowered opponents with their serves and baseline shots. They could also run down balls with their speed.

Venus was the first to break through. She beat fellow US player Lindsay Davenport in the finals in 2000 and captured her second crown the following year. But Serena was not to be outdone. All eyes were on Serena when she met her older sister for the 2002 title. People in the United States who had lost interest in women's tennis were paying attention when Venus and Serena clashed that year.

The sisters battled to a first-set tiebreaker. Serena took control of the match with her hustle. Venus dinked a shot just over the net that most others would never have reached. But Serena not only got to it, she also flicked it past Venus to win the point. She then smashed an ace that whizzed by Venus at 100 miles per hour. Serena had won the first set.

There was no stopping Serena after that. Venus was nursing a sore right shoulder. She was no match for her sister. Soon Serena was celebrating her first Wimbledon title. And Venus was lamenting her first Wimbledon finals defeat. But it was not like other defeats. After all, she loved the young woman who beat her.

"It's definitely a different feeling from playing some other players," Venus said. "Serena is my sister and I'm really happy she won, especially

Unusual Trophy

The women's singles champion at Wimbledon does not raise a trophy in the air. She has received the Venus Rosewater Dish since 1886. The dish is made of sterling silver and trimmed in gold. After it is presented, it is returned to the Wimbledon Lawn Tennis Museum. The winner gets to keep an eight-inch replica.

for the first time. I would have loved to have won, but at the same time, I'm so happy for her."

The Williams sisters were just warming up. Venus won three more singles titles and Serena won four through 2012. They entertained millions of fans everywhere by clashing in the 2002, 2003, 2008, and 2009 finals. Serena won three of those matches. After Serena won again in 2012, each sister had five Wimbledon singles titles.

Fabulous Federer

Once Sampras retired in 2002, US dominance in men's singles became a distant memory. The only bright light was power-hitting Andy Roddick, who reached the finals in 2004, 2005, and 2009. But he fell to Swiss star Roger Federer all three times.

Roger Federer serves to Andy Roddick of the United States during the 2009 Wimbledon men's final. Federer beat Roddick for the title in 2004, 2005, and 2009.

Roddick won his first set against Federer in a Wimbledon final in 2004 before losing six straight through 2004 and 2005. But in 2009, Roddick battled Federer for five sets and more than four hours. The epic title match was among the most dramatic in Wimbledon history.

The Wimbledon rule banning tiebreakers in the fifth set heightened the tension. Brilliant shot was followed by brilliant shot. Well into the fifth hour of battle, the two stars were still dead even. The marathon fifth set was tied at 14–14.

Federer won the next game. But there was no reason to believe he could break Roddick's serve to win the match. He had not broken the powerful Roddick serve all day. It seemed the match might continue

Three Days, One Match

Few paid attention when little-known players John Isner and Nicolas Mahut began their first-round Wimbledon match on June 22, 2010. There was nothing unusual when the two battled to a 6–6 tie in the fifth set. There was nothing even too unusual when darkness forced the match to be postponed. But something very unusual happened when Isner and Mahut returned the next day. They played for more than seven hours and never broke serve.

With the fifth set tied at an amazing 59–59 score, darkness again prevailed. The two returned for a third day before Isner broke serve and won the fifth set, 70–68. The fifth set alone lasted eight hours and 11 minutes. That was two hours longer than any match in Wimbledon history.

"We played the greatest match ever in the greatest place to play tennis," Mahut said. "I thought [Isner] would make a mistake. I waited for that moment, and it never came."

into the night. But suddenly Roddick lost his booming serve. He lost his forehand. After two unforced errors, he had also lost the longest fifth set in Wimbledon history. And he had lost the match.

Federer had won his fifteenth Grand Slam event, breaking the mark set by Sampras. Roddick understood what that record meant to his US friend. He wished he could have prevented it from being broken.

"Sorry, Pete, I tried to hold him off," Roddick said as he held back tears. "It was great to play Roger, a great champion."

Federer remained a great champion. But he was no

longer unbeatable. Rafael Nadal of Spain had proven that in the 2008 Wimbledon finals. And young Serbian star Novak Djokovic soon emerged as a third tennis superstar. He easily beat Nadal to win the 2011 title. But Federer then won his seventh title in 2012, tying Renshaw and Sampras for most all-time Wimbledon titles.

Nobody can predict the future winners at Wimbledon. But it is easy to predict that it will continue to be the greatest event in tennis.

TIMELINE

Major Walter Clopton Wingfield introduces his sport of lawn tennis at a party.

1873

Spencer Gore defeats W. C. Marshall to win the first Wimbledon singles title on July 19.

1877

William Renshaw defeats brother Ernest on July 13 to win the last of his seven Wimbledon singles championships.

1889

Wimbledon adds foreign players and becomes an international tournament.

1901

Laurie Doherty beats Frank Riseley on July 5, concluding a run of nine Wimbledon singles titles in 10 years for Doherty brothers Laurie and Reginald.

1906

The Open Era of tennis begins as paid players are allowed to participate at Wimbledon and other events.

1968

Nearly 100 men's players boycott Wimbledon to protest the banning of Yugoslavian star Nikki Pilic.

1973

Young Jimmy Connors dominates veteran Rosewall in the Wimbledon final on July 6 to usher in a new era of tennis.

1974

Arthur Ashe becomes the first black male singles champion at Wimbledon by upsetting Jimmy Connors in the finals on July 5.

1975

Upstart Martina Navratilova wins the first of her record nine Wimbledon singles titles on July 7 by beating Chris Evert in the finals for the first of five times.

1978

1924

Four French men known as "The Four Musketeers" begin dominating Wimbledon singles and doubles. Their reign lasts through 1929.

1938

Helen Wills Moody captures the last of her eight Wimbledon singles championships on July 2 by beating Helen Jacobs in the finals for the fourth time.

1940

Wimbledon is canceled due to World War II. German bombs fall on Centre Court in 1940. The tournament resumes in 1946.

1956

Lew Hoad kicks off an era of Australian dominance by beating fellow Australian Ken Rosewall in the Wimbledon men's singles final on July 6.

1957

Althea Gibson becomes the first black Wimbledon singles champion by defeating Darlene Hard on July 6.

1980

Swedish sensation Bjorn Borg beats John McEnroe in one of the most epic Wimbledon singles finals in history on July 5.

1998

Pete Sampras wins a classic power matchup against Goran Ivanisevic in a five-set final on July 5. It is one of his seven Wimbledon singles titles.

2000

Venus Williams begins an era of dominance by the Williams sisters by beating Lindsay Davenport in the Wimbledon singles finals on July 16.

2008

Rafael Nadal beats Roger Federer in a nearly five-hour Wimbledon singles final classic on July 6.

2012

In beating Andy Murray, Federer ties Sampras and Renshaw in winning his record seventh men's singles title.

CHAMPIONSHIP OVERVIEW

The Trophy

The Gentlemen's Singles Trophy has been awarded since 1887, while the Venus Rosewater Dish has gone to the women's champion since 1886.

The Legends

Bjorn Borg (Sweden): Five singles titles in a row from 1976 to 1980.

Roger Federer (Switzerland): Seven singles titles from 2003 to 2012.

Billie Jean King (United States): Six singles, 10 doubles, and four mixed doubles titles from 1961 to 1979.

Martina Navratilova (Czechoslovakia/ United States): Nine singles, seven doubles, and four mixed doubles titles from 1976 to 2003.

The Venue

The All England Lawn Tennis and Croquet Club has been home to Wimbledon since the beginning, in 1877, and has been an influential center of tennis ever since. The club moved to its current location in southwest London in 1922. Among the noteworthy traditions maintained at the All England Club over the years are its iconic grass courts, limited advertising, strawberries and cream, and all-white dress code among players.

GLOSSARY

ace

A serve in play that is untouched by an opponent.

amateur

An athlete who is not allowed to earn money for playing.

break

To win a game against an opponent's serve.

championship point

A point that would give a player the championship if won.

Grand Slam

The four major tournaments played every year: Australian Open, French Open, Wimbledon, US Open.

match point

A point that could clinch a victory in a match.

tiebreaker

An addition to a set played when the score is tied at 6–6. The first player to reach seven points, and lead by two points, wins the tiebreaker and set.

topspin

A groundstroke on which a player hits on top of the ball to push it forward and make it jump faster and harder when it lands.

unforced errors

Points lost due to a mistake, such as hitting the ball into the net.

union

A group of people who join together to better defend their interests.

FOR MORE INFORMATION

Selected Bibliography

Collins, Bud. *History of Tennis*. Chicago: New Chapter Press, 2010.

Cronin, Matthew. *Epic: John McEnroe, Bjorn Borg, and the Greatest Tennis Season Ever*. Hoboken, N.J.: John Wiley & Sons, 2011.

Green, David. *101 Reasons to Love the Greatest Tournament in Tennis*. New York: Stewart, Tabori & Chang, 2011.

Medlycott, James. *100 Years of The Wimbledon Tennis Championships*. Great Britain: Crescent Books, 1977.

Further Readings

Glaser, Jason. *Roger Federer (Today's Sports Greats)*. New York: Gareth Stevens Publishing, 2011.

Hewitt, Ian and Martin, Bob. *Wimbledon: Visions of The Championships*. London: Vision Sports Publishing, 2011.

Kubik, Jeff. *Wimbledon (Sporting Championships)*. New York: Weigl Publishers, 2007.

Sandler, Michael. *Tennis: Victory for Venus Williams (Upsets & Comebacks)*. New York: Bearport Publishing, 2006.

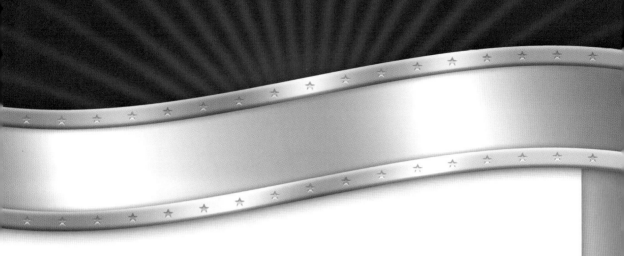

Web Links

To learn more about Wimbledon, visit ABDO Publishing Company online at **www.abdopublishing.com**. Web sites about Wimbledon are featured on our Book Links page. These links are routinely monitored and updated to provide the most current information available.

Places to Visit

All England Lawn Tennis and Croquet Club
Church Road
Wimbledon, London, UK SW19 5AE
+44 (0)20 8944 1066
www.wimbledon.com/en_GB/about_aeltc/index.html
The All England Club has been at the center of tennis since it hosted the first Wimbledon in 1877. The club features a museum about the history of Wimbledon and lawn tennis as well as guided tours.

International Tennis Hall of Fame Museum
194 Bellevue Avenue, Newport, RI 02840
(401) 849-3990
www.tennisfame.com
The museum chronicles more than eight centuries of tennis history through interactive exhibits, videos, and memorabilia. The grounds also feature 13 grass tennis courts.

INDEX

About the Author

Marty Gitlin is a freelance writer and author. He won more than 45 writing awards as a newspaper journalist, including first place for general excellence from Associated Press in 1995. That organization also voted him as one of the top four feature writers in Ohio in 2001. Gitlin lives with his wife and three kids in Cleveland, Ohio.